THE BEST (AND WORST) COW JOKES EVER!

Illustrations drawn by @Atolonia_
Cover Design and book design by Paul-Hawkins.com

All rights reserved. Text and images copyright Mark Pallis.
This book or any portion thereof may not be reproduced or used in any manner whatsoever without the express written permission of the publisher except for the use of brief excerpts in a review.

First Printing, 2022
ISBN: 978-1-915337-45-0
MarkPallis.com

Are you ready to be a<u>moo</u>sed? All set to laugh at some <u>udderly</u> ridiculous cow jokes? Well, you've come to the right place.

This, my friends, is an entire book of cow jokes! Yes, you heard that right: 100% cow.

There's old favourites, there's some new favourites - let's call them 'future classics'! And if that wasn't enough, there are also some very special 'niche' jokes.

When something is 'niche', it means that it's particular: not for everyone. So be warned, not everyone will laugh at the niche jokes. In fact, most people will probably go 'Huh?' But then you'll explain and they'll go, "Ah, I see!" And of course, *someone* will laugh (even if it's just you and me!).

You'll also see that on every page, there are little explanations for each joke. Some of them might seem pretty obvious, but that's probably because you're really clever!

The reason the explanations are there is because, for me, there is nothing more annoying than a joke that you don't get. So, in this book, you'll never have to say "I don't get it", because every joke is explained! Awesome!

How to write your own cow jokes

There's only one rule in comedy. And that's that there are no rules! So with that in mind, you'll be glad to know that it is easy to write your own jokes. Here's how moo can do it, sorry, how you can do it.

Start with the punchline (the punchline is that last line of the joke - it's the part that has the funny bit in it).

Think of some words that have a 'moo' sound in them – or a sound that is pretty close to 'moo'. Moody. Mobile. Museum. Music. And that's step one.

Next, replace that sound with 'Moo'. So: Moody, Moobile, Mooseum, Moosic. There we go, that's your punchline sorted. Now you know how the joke is going to end.

But of course, if you just say, 'The cow ate Mooseli", that's not funny. You need a 'set up'. The set up is the first line of the joke. Here's how I do it. I say to myself, "Hmm, what kind of a question could you ask where 'Museli' is the answer?

Then you say... Hmm, what about "What do cows have for breakfast? Or "What do cows eat for breakfast?" Or 'What's a cow's favourite breakfast". Boom! There it is! You have your set up, you have your punchline... You are a comedian, or should we say, a COWmedian!?!

If you want to do more jokes, you can think of other features of a cow and make up some jokes about those things. So, what do we know about cows? They have horns. They make milk. They eat grass or hay. Hmmm. How could you turn those things into jokes? Over to you!!

Don't forget, there is no right or wrong answer! If you think it's funny, the chances are, someone else will too. So go for it!

And guess what, there's another bonus too. Playing around with words like this encourages something called Verbal Dexterity. What that means, basically, is that the more jokes you read and the more jokes you come up with, the more you become a Word Jedi! You can control words, play with them. Their master you will be!

What are you waiting for, let's get a moove on...

CONTENTS

Chapter One: .... Cow jokes

Chapter Two: .... More cow jokes

Chapter Three: .... Even more cow jokes

Chapter Four: .... Guess what? It's cow jokes

Chapter Five: .... Jokes about cows

Chapter Six: .... One last cow joke

CHAPTER 1

Cow jokes

What did one cow
say to the other?

"I LIKE THE WAY
YOU **MOO**VE!"

moove = move

Why can cows
dance so well?

THEY HAVE
GREAT **MOO**VES!

What is a cow's favourite instrument?

THE HORN!

Cows have horns.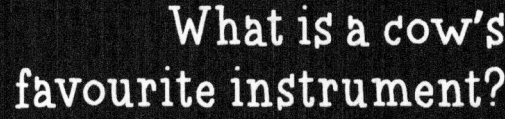

A horn is also a type of instrument that you blow...

How do cows talk to their friends?

WITH A MOOBILE PHONE!

moobile phone = mobile phone

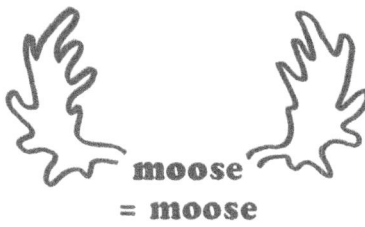

moose = moose

When is a cow not a cow?
WHEN IT'S A MOOSE!

How did the cow get ahead at work?

SHE WAS GREAT AT AT SCHMOOZING!

When someone is good at 'schmoozing', they talk to others to impress them or get something

What's a cow's favourite seafood?

MOOLES!

Mooles = Moules

(Moules, or 'moules marinière' are a special seafood that comes in a black shell)

Why was the cow grumpy?

IT WAS IN A BAD MOOD!

mood = mood

Where do cows go to learn about history?

TO THE MOOSEUM!

mooseum = museum

CHAPTER 2

More cow jokes

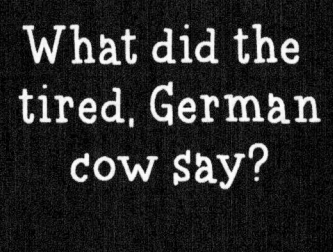

What did the tired, German cow say?

"ICH BiN MOO-DE!"

In German, if you are tired, you say: "Ich bin müde"

(Müde sounds like **moo-de**)

Who is a cow's favourite English playwright?

NOEL COWARD

Who is a cow's favourite French philosopher?

ALBERT CAMOO

Albert Camoo = Albert Camus

Who is a cow's second favourite French philosopher

MICHEL FOUCOW

Michel Foucow = Michel Foucault

Why are cows so good at mindfulness?

THEY ARE ALWAYS IN THE MOOMENT!

moooment = moment

(Mindfulness is all about being in the moment)

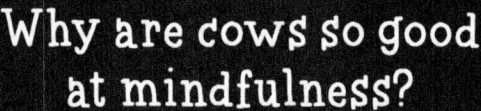

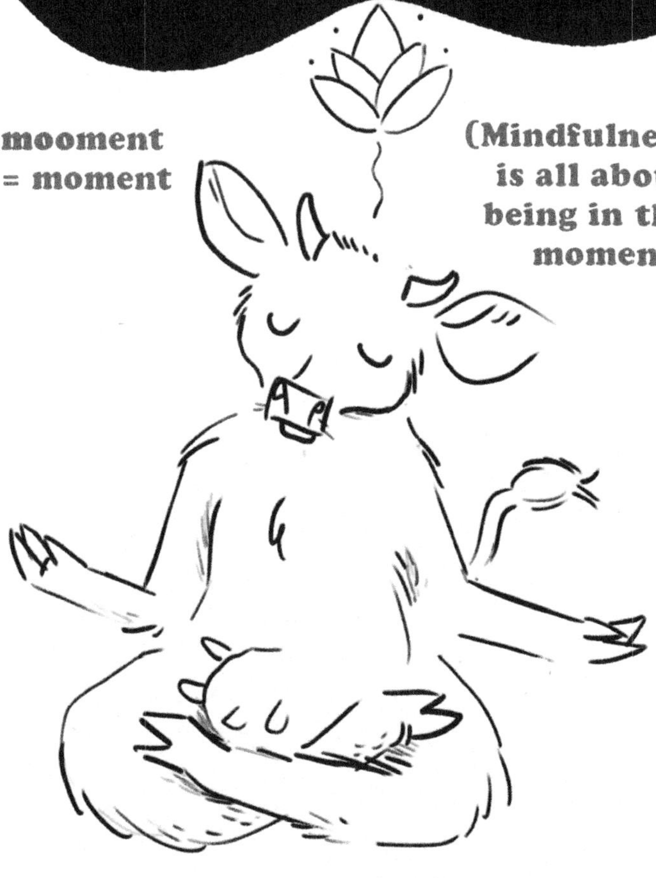

How do you tell a cow to go away?

SAY "VA-MOOSE!"

Vomoose is a word that's a bit like 'scram' or 'get out of here'

What's a cow's favourite dance step?

THE MOONWALK!

What's a cow's favourite website?

MOOTUBE!

MooTube = YouTube

How do you move a cow?

SAY "MOOVE!"

moove = move

What is a cow's favourite mathmatical challenge?

MOOLTIPLICATION!

mooltiplication = multiplication

What's another name for a Australian cow?

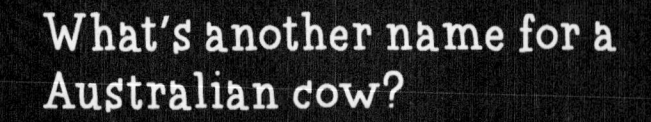

A COW FROM DOWN **UDDER!**

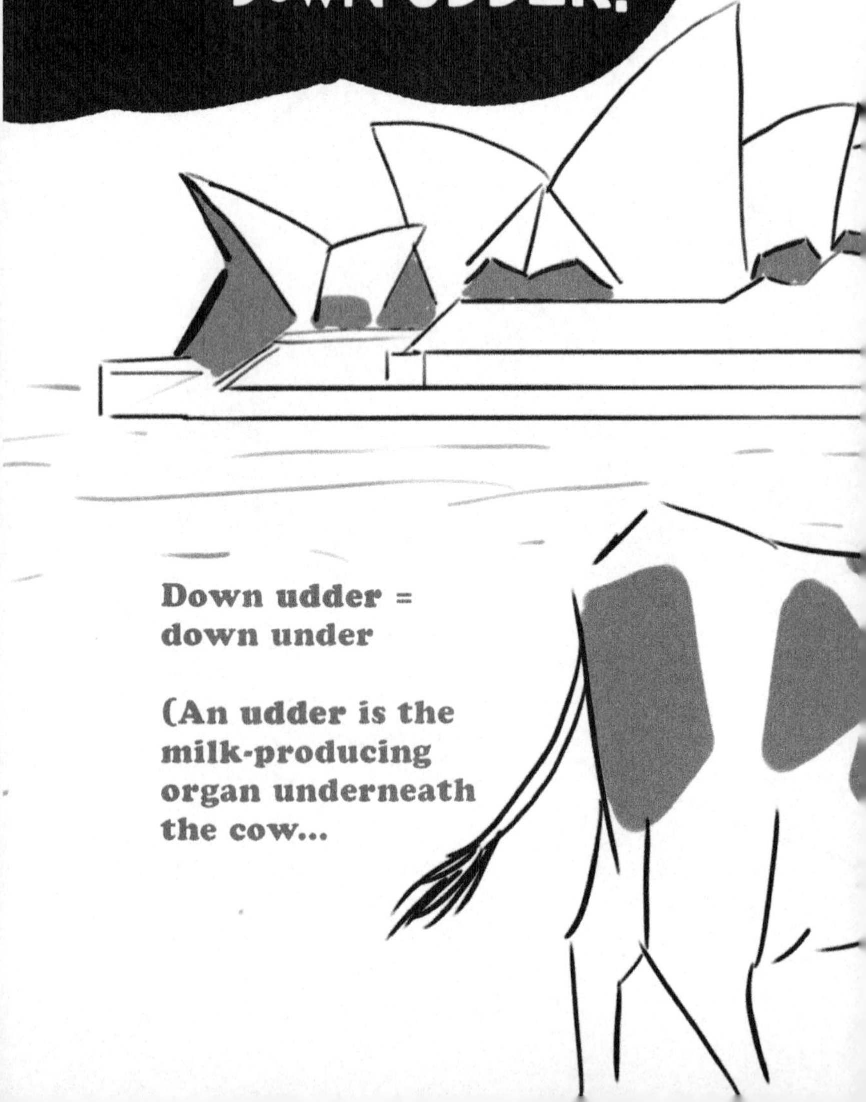

Down udder = down under

(An udder is the milk-producing organ underneath the cow...

camooflage = camouflage

Why couldn't you see the cow?

IT HAD CAMOOFLAGE!

... and people talk about Australia as the land 'down under' because it is below the equator.)

CHAPTER 3

Even more cow jokes

What do cows say when they dance?

"I LiKE TO **MOOVE** iT, **MOOVE** iT!"

moosic = music

Why did the cows dance?

BECAUSE THEY HEARD **MOO**SiC!

What is a cow's favourite party game?

MOOSiCAL CHAiRS!

moosical = musical

What did one cow's tail say to the other cow's tail?

"YOU LOOK **SWISH!**"

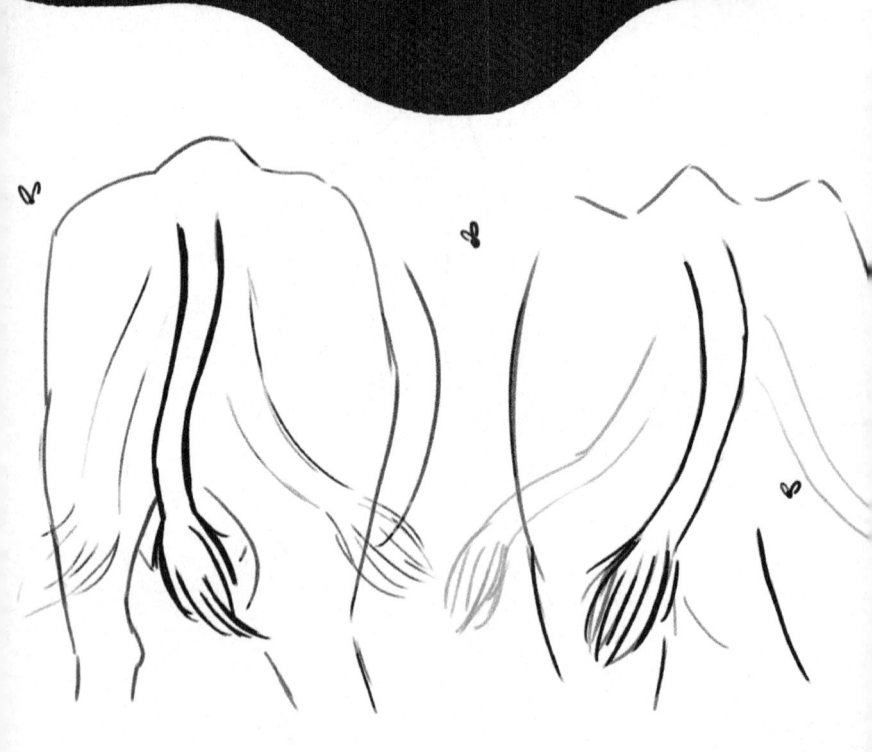

"KNOCK, KNOCK?"

Who's there?

"COWS GO."

Cows go who?

"NO! COWS GO MOO!"

←

When a cow's tail swings, people say it goes 'swish'.

But also, if you 'look swish' that means you look good!

Why do cows love maths?

BECAUSE THEY'RE GOOD AT COWNTING!

cownting = counting

Why do cows love sums like 3 x 2 = 6 and 2 x 3 = 6?

BECAUSE THEY LOVE COMOOTATIVITY!

comootativity = commutativity.

(Commutativity is when you add or multiply numbers and get the same answer, no matter what order the numbers are in.)

A-cow-ntant = accountant

(An accountant is someone that sorts out your money and taxes.)

Who sorts out a cow's money?

THEiR A-**COW**-NTANT!

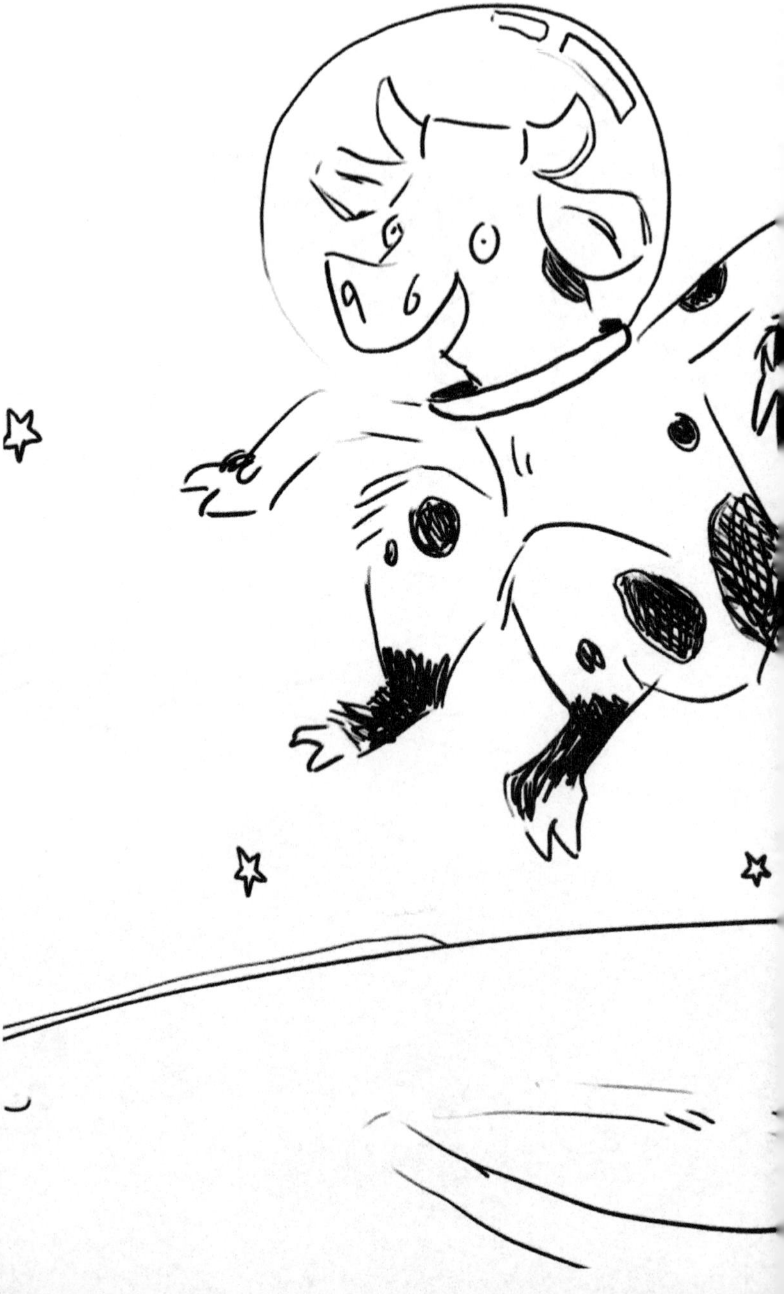

Where did the first cow in space go?

TO THE MOON!

moon = moon

What is a cow's favourite city?

MOO YORK!

Moo York = New York

What is a cow's second favourite city?

MOONICH!

What is a cow's third favourite city?

MosCOW!

Moonich = Munich

What's a cow's favourite country?

BULL-GARIA!

Bull-garia = Bulgaria

What's a cow's second favourite country?

MOO ZEALAND

Moo Zealand = New Zealand

How did Roman cows decorate their floors?

WiTH MOOSAiCS!

moosaic = mosaic

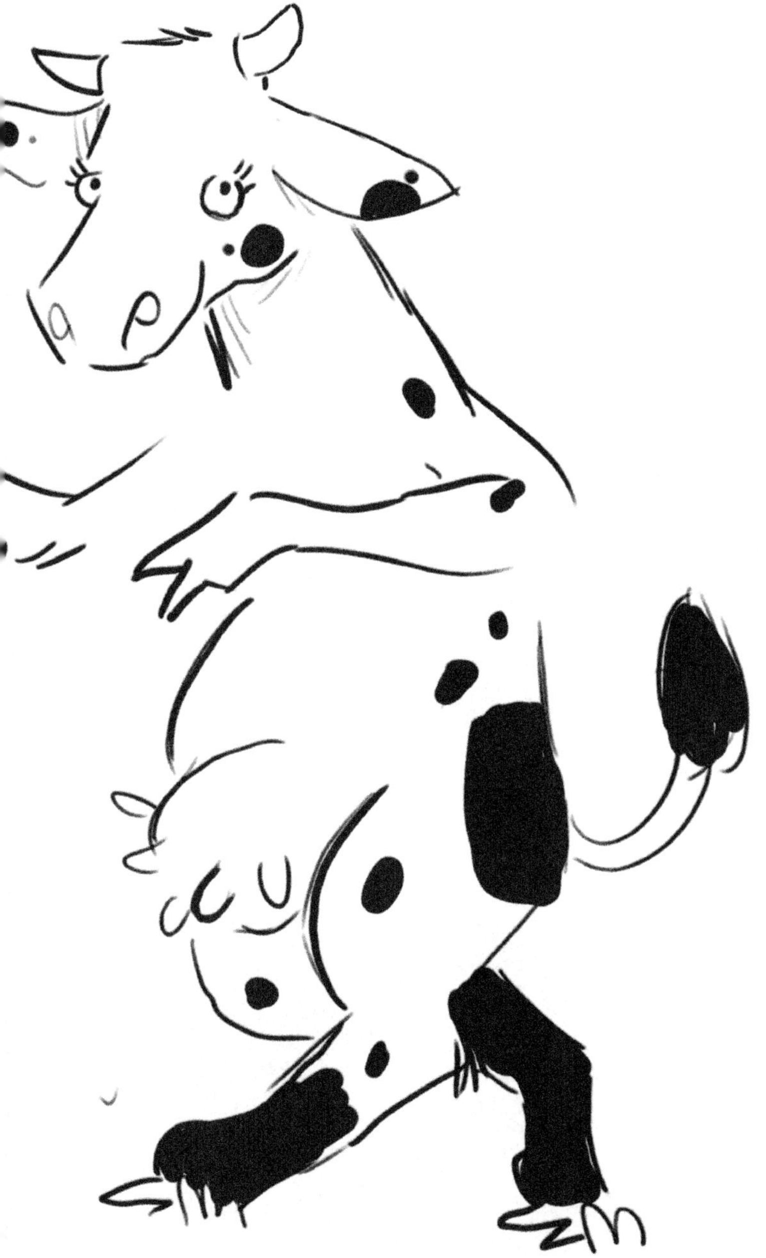

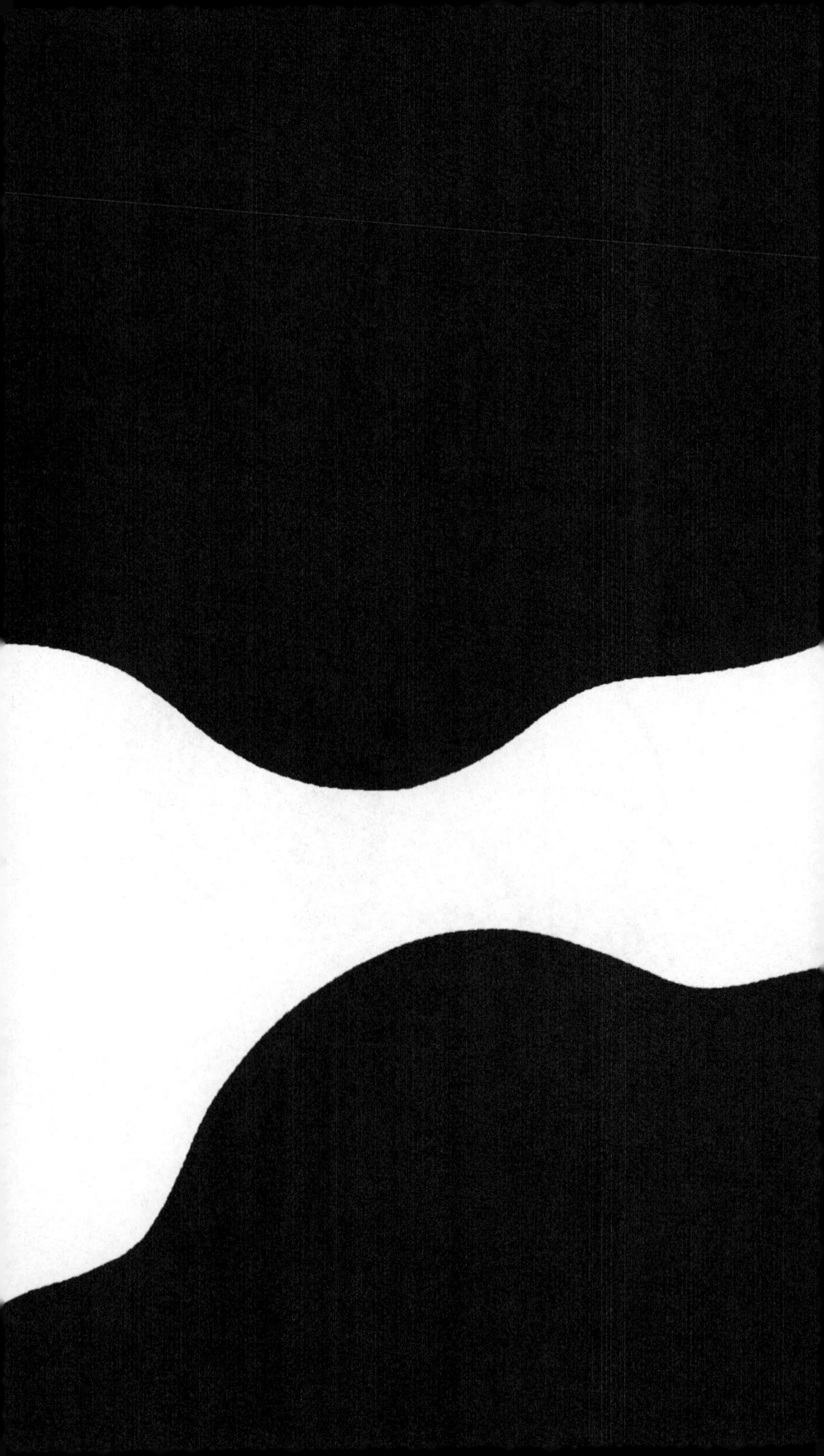

CHAPTER 4

Guess what? It's cow jokes

Why don't cows have beards?

THEY PREFER MOOSTACHES!

moostaches = mustaches

How did the cow feel when he shaved off his MOOstache?

sMOOTH

A mustache makes your face prickly. When you shave it off, your face is smooth again.

How do you say "Thanks very much" to a Spanish cow?

"MOOCHAS GRACIAS!"

Moochas gracias = muchas gracias

('Muchas gracias' means 'thank you very much' in Spanish.)

How do German cows
say thank you?

THEY SAY "DAN-**KUH!**"

In German, 'danke' means 'thanks'.

(It is pronounced, *'dan-kuh.'* And, the German word 'Kuh' means 'Cow'.)

What do German cows call their mummies?

MOOTi!

In German, 'mummy' is 'Mutti,' which is pronounced Mooti!

How did the bull drink his tea?

WITHOUT MILK!

You can drink your tea with milk, or without.

Bulls don't make milk, so if you are a bull, you can't put your own milk in your own tea!

Why does a bull eat his cereal dry?

BECAUSE HE'S GOT NO MILK!

What can't a bull get a job as a milkman?

BECAUSE HE NEVER HAS ANY MILK!

What do you call a cow who isn't brave?

A COWARD!

A 'coward' is a word to describe a person who isn't brave

What did the rich cow say?

I'VE GOT LOADS OF MOOLAH!

Moolah = moolah

(Moolah is a slang way of saying money.)

What does a cow call the people that it works with?

COWoRKERS!

coworkers = co-workers

(A 'co-worker' is what you call a person that you work with.)

Where do trendy cows go to work?

A COWoRKiNG SPACE!

How do cows get to work?

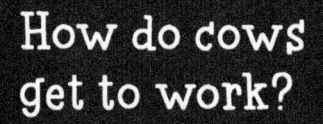

THEY COMMOOTE!

commoote = commute. (Commuting is the word to describe a journey to work.)

co-working space = co-working space

(A 'co-working space' is a shared office. They are normally pretty cool and trendy.)

Where do cows go to get their medicine?

THE **FARM**acy!

farmacy = pharmacy

(Pharmacies are where you get medicine. Cows live on farms.)

Why did the cow cross the road?

To GET TO THE **UDDER** SiDE!

Moonlight Sonata is a famous, calming piece of piano music by Ludvig van Beethoven

What is a cow's favourite piece of classical music?

MOONLIGHT SONATA!

CHAPTER 5

Jokes about cows

What do you call a cow who stars in films?

A **MOOViE STAR!**

moovie = movie

What did the boastful cow say to its friends?

"MY MILK IS LEGEN**DAIRY**!"

legendairy = legendary

(Cows that give milk are called dairy cows. And it's a bit boastful to call yourself legendary!)

What do you call a cow who tells jokes?

A **COW**MEDIAN!

cowmedian = comedian

How do you wish 'Happy Birthday' to a young female cow?

YOU SAY 'HEIFER HAPPY BIRTHDAY'

heifer = 'have a'

(A 'heifer' is what you call a young female cow.)

Why did the farmer put their cow on a trampoline?

THEY WANTED MILKSHAKE!

This is funny because you would never put a cow on a trampoline, and even if you did, it would not make a milkshake!

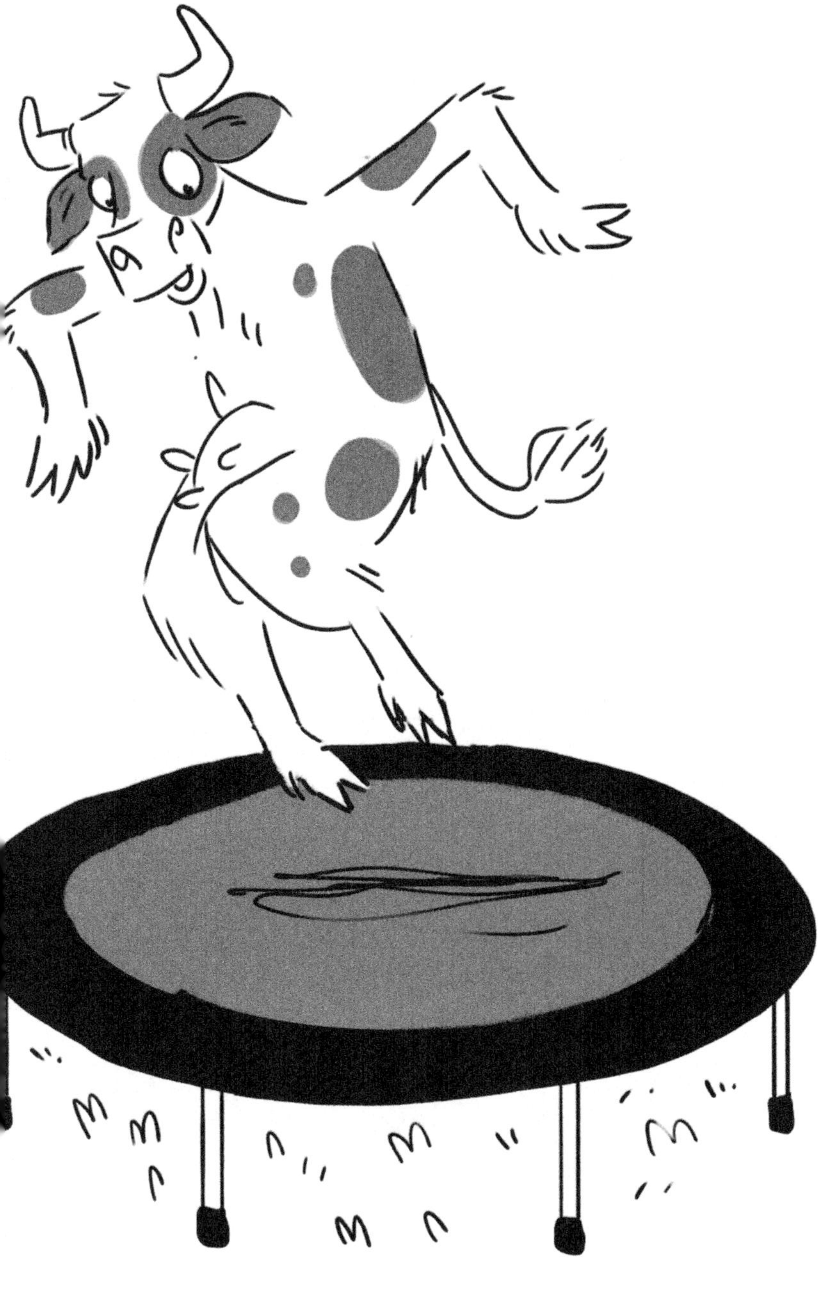

What did the buffalo say to its son when they went to school?

"BISON!"

bison = "bye son"

(A bison is also known as a buffalo.)

How do cows cut their grass?

WITH A LAWNMOOER!

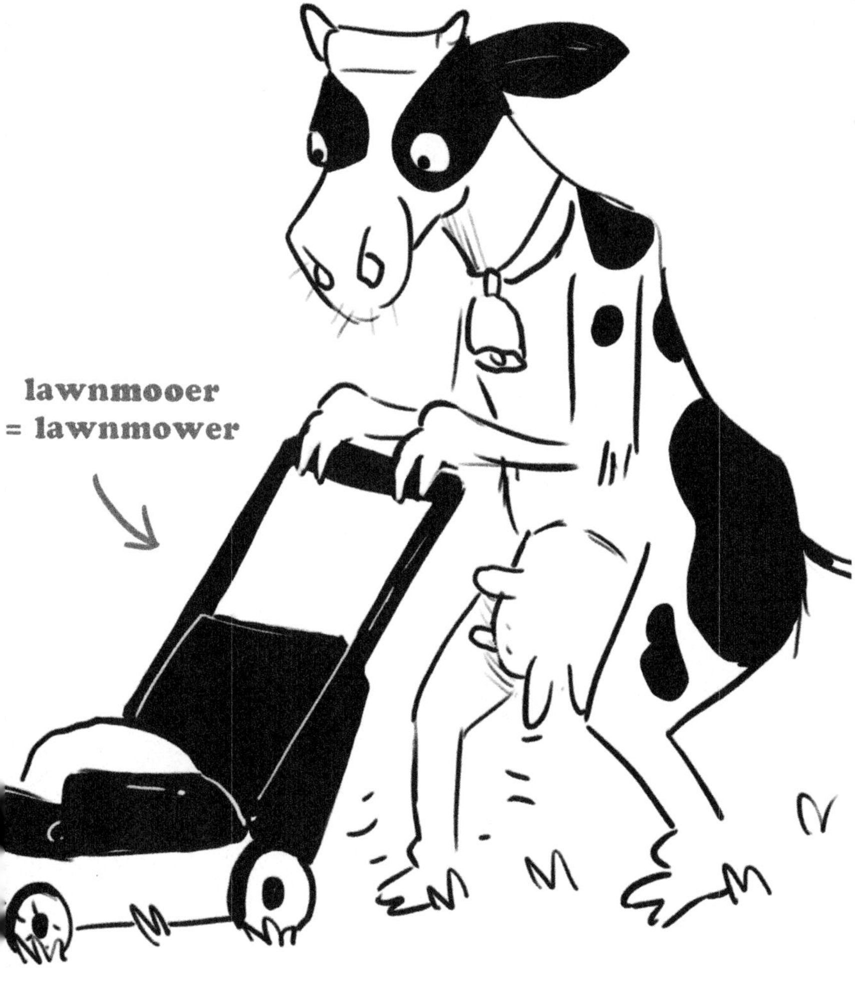
lawnmooer
= lawnmower

Why was the cow wearing headphones?

IT WAS LISTENING TO **MOO**SIC!

What do you call a cow who watches too much TV?

A **COW**CH POTATO!

(A couch potato is what you call someone who watches so much TV, they basically are just like a potato sitting on the sofa.)

Why didn't the cow sit on the chair?

cowch = couch

IT PREFERRED THE **COW**CH!

How do cows relax?

THEY GO TO THE MOOVIES!

moovies = movies

Why was the cow bald?

remooval = removal

IT USED TOO MUCH HAIR REMOOVAL CREAM!

How do naughty cows laugh?

THEY SAY "MOO HA HA!"

'Moo ha ha' is the sound that baddies sometimes make when they laugh in cartoons

Why are cows so good at dancing?

THEY'VE GOT THE BEST MOOVES!

How does a cow make the TV go quiet?

THEY USE THE MOOT BUTTON!

moot = mute

(You press the mute button on a remote control to make the TV go quiet.)

What does a cow say to make its lunch appear by magic?

"HAY PRESTO!"

Hay presto = Hey Presto

(Cows eat hay, and 'hey presto' is one of those words like abracadabra.)

Where do cows go after they get married?

ON HONEYMOON!

'Honeymoon' is the name of the special holiday that people take after they get married

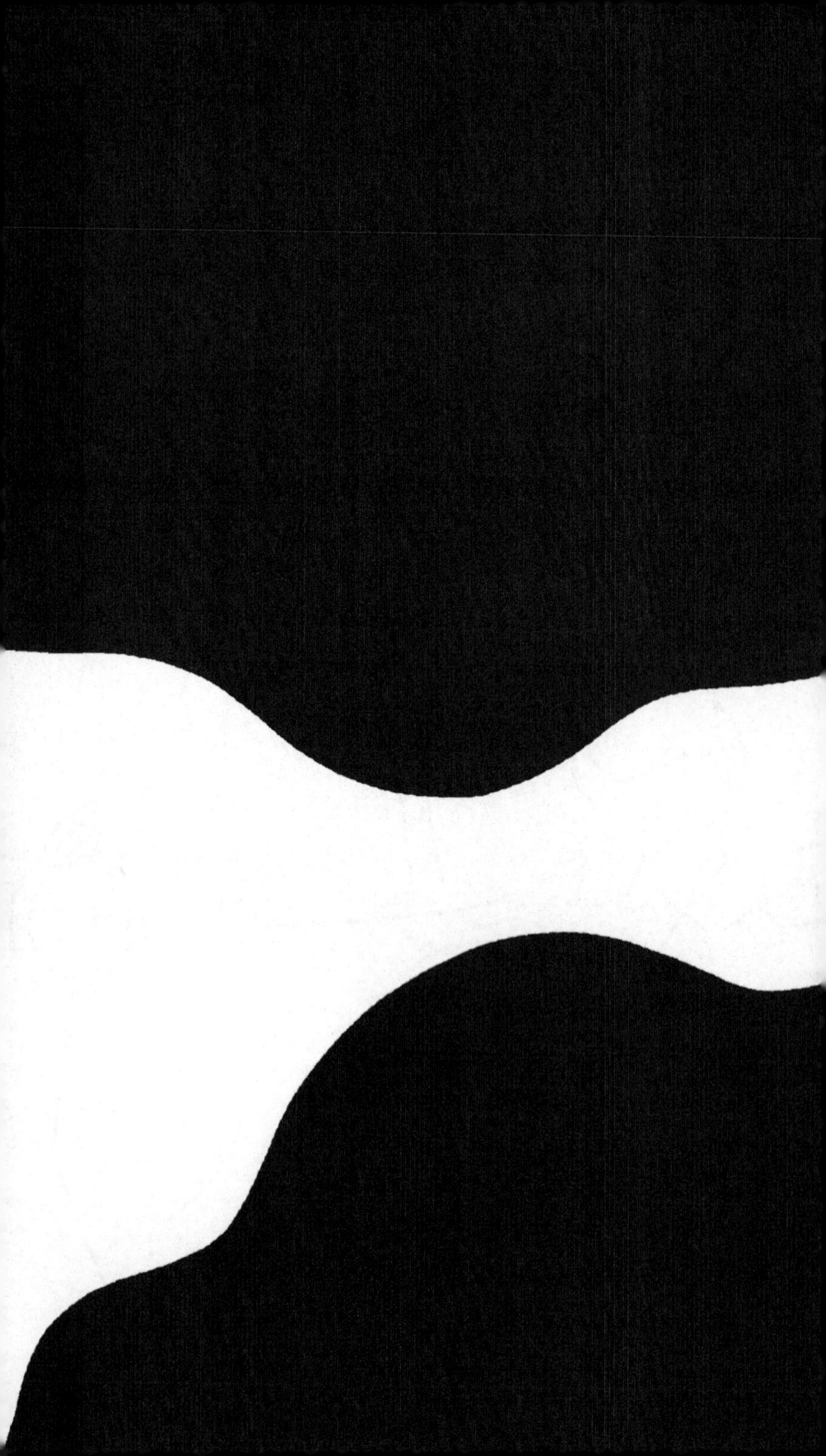

CHAPTER 6

One more cow joke

Why do I only tell cow jokes?

I DON'T KNOW ANY **UDDER** ONES!

Bill Gates, the billionaire and philanthropist apparently said "We all need people who will give us feedback. That's how we improve." I want to improve, so whatever you thought of the jokes, please let me and others know by leaving a review on Amazon or Goodreads or any other favourite site!

What was the best joke? What was the worst? What should the next joke book be about? Every review will help make the next book funnier!

Thanks very moo-ch!

Are you ready for......

The best (and worst) Book Jokes Ever!

I STEAL MONEY BY ROBIN BANKS

the funniest Joke books in the world!

← This is a 'book joke'!

FOR BIG KIDS, LITTLE KIDS, AND PUN-LOVING GROWN-UPS!

THE BEST (AND WORST) BOOK JOKES EVER!

Simple maths
by
Zoe Zee

Got to go
by
Sia Layder

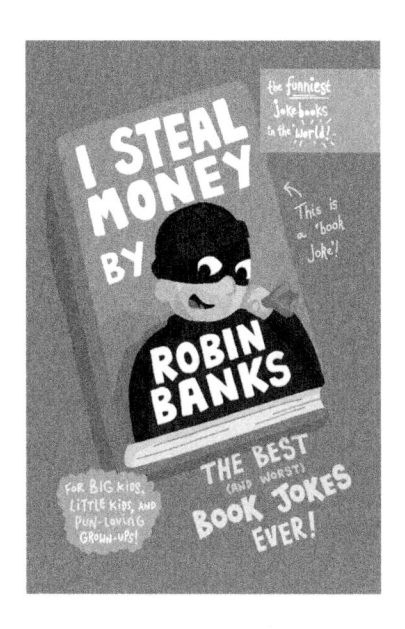

**Zoe Zee = So easy
Simple maths questions like
1+1 really are so easy!**

**Sia Layder = See you later.
Bye bye!**

Includes explanations so you can be sure to 'get' every joke.

More books to enjoy from NEU WESTEND — PRESS —

Learning languages just got fun!

An additional language opens a child's mind, broadens their horizons and enriches their emotional life. Research has shown that the time between a child's birth and their sixth or seventh birthday is a "golden period" when they are most receptive to new languages. These books subtly blend 50 words in a new language into a fun and heartwarming story. Children learn without realising!

Available in more than 50 languages, from French and Italian, to Hebrew, Ukrainian and Latin!

www.markpallis.com

Do you call them hugs or cuddles?

In this funny, heartwarming rhyming story, you will laugh out loud as two loveable gibbons try to figure out if a hug is better than a cuddle and, in the process, learn how to get along.

Crab and Whale is the best-selling story of how a little Crab helps a big Whale. It's carefully designed to help even the most energetic children find a moment of calm and focus. It also includes a special mindful breathing exercise and affirmation for children.

One of Mindful.org's 'Seven Mindful Children's books'

NEU WESTEND
— PRESS —